AF808901

CALIFORNIA STATE PRISON MUGSHOTS

Eric "Superman" Sturgess

Rose Of Sharon
PUBLISHING

ERIC "SUPERMAN" STURGESS

Printed Worldwide
First Printing 2025
First Edition 2025

10 9 8 7 6 5 4 3 2 1

Rose of Sharon Publishing books may be ordered through booksellers or by contacting:

Rose Of Sharon Publishing
roseofsharonpublishing.com
P.O. Box 186
Floresville, Texas 78114

ISBN: 978-1-970335-21-7 Paperback

Dedication

This book is a heartfelt dedication to the men in the California Department of Corrections and Rehabilitation, as well as those in prisons across America, who are striving to improve themselves and reunite with their loved ones. Within the confines of those prison walls, many men have been blessed with remarkable talents, and they take great pride in their creations and the stories they have to share. This humble book serves as a platform for their voices to be heard.

I have taken it upon myself to write numerous letters of support for resentencing and parole board hearings on behalf of my incarcerated friends in the California Department of Corrections and Rehabilitation. I am fully committed to assisting in their release, and these letters of support play a crucial role in that endeavor.

"The Lord has given them special skills as engravers, designers, embroiderers in blue, purple, and scarlet thread on fine linen cloth, and weavers. They excel as craftsmen and as designers," Exodus 35:35.

God bless you,
Eric "Superman" Sturgess
Psalm 91

Preface

California state prison mugshot photos are taken when an individual first enters the prison system. These photos are used for their identification cards. Convicts receive one upon arrival at the reception center, and then they are issued a different one upon transfer to the specific prison to which they are assigned. After that, they are exchanged when they become old, when they are lost, or when the convict undergoes physical changes. New pictures for the identification cards are taken every few years.

I have been collecting prison identification cards of convicts in the California Department of Corrections and Rehabilitation for several years now. They are rare and hard to find. These photos and the men in them deserve to be seen by others and their lives not forgotten in the dustbins of history. It just reminds us how fleeting our lives are. Nobody is guaranteed tomorrow, and our youth quickly fades to old age if we are blessed to live that long.

God bless you
Eric Sturgess
Romans 10:9-13

Foreword

The prison community is not much different than any other community in and around the world. We, as incarcerated individuals, have to abide by rules and regulations, as well as the positive or negative norms, values, and principles that influence our daily lives.

Our ID cards are, and play a vital role in our daily prison life. These ID cards are similar to the IDs and driver's licenses people use in the free world. They provide us with access to multiple buildings within the prison, including the law library, school, vocational areas, kitchen, yard, gym, cell blocks, family visit areas, and medical facilities, among others.

Our IDs are essential because without them, we cannot move around, buy groceries at the prison canteen store, receive medical treatment, packages, or even log into our tablets or use the phone.

In the past, our ID cards were available in various colors, including red, blue, and green. Each color represented a different classification status. For instance, the red privilege card (A1A Assigned) was given to convicts when they were assigned to a job, vocational trade, or school. This card provided individuals with access to additional prison activities, including the gym, as well as the weekend and nighttime yard. It also allowed individuals to spend more money at the canteen store and use the phone once a day.

The blue card was given to individuals classified as A2B. The privilege of individuals with blue cards was a little more restricted, as they were not allowed to go out at night or enter other areas within the prison. Individuals classified as A2B were provided with one phone call per month, which had to be made within the first ten days of the month.

The green card was distributed to individuals who were A1A unassigned. Meaning they had the same privileges as those with red cards but lacked a job assignment. Therefore, there were areas within the prison that they were unable to access.

The red, blue, and green card system was discontinued in some prisons in the early 2000s. However, some prisons continued to carry them up to 2007 or even longer. Today, our cards are the same for everyone. They are mainly white with green tones. They display our last name, first name, CDCR number, PID number, the date the ID was issued, and our date of birth. It also shows a barcode that can be scanned by medical staff and other officials, if necessary, to verify our identity.

This may sound far-fetched, but as in the free world, there have been cases of mistaken identity, as well as stolen identity, within the prison system. I have personally witnessed individuals claiming and receiving packages, store, and even personal mail that belongs to others. This tends to happen mostly to convicts who possess the same last name or whose last names are too common.

Therefore, due to the above, CDCR title 15. 3019 states the following: "Inmates must carry on their person any identification card issued for identification purposes, in accordance with institution procedures. Inmates must not mutilate or destroy such cards nor possess the card of another inmate. An inmate must surrender their identification card or cards upon request by any employee. Unless a card is being officially recalled, the card(s) will be promptly returned to the inmate when the staff member's use of the card has been completed. An inmate may be charged for the replacement of a deliberately mutilated, lost, or destroyed card in accordance with section 3011. An inmate may also be charged for the replacement of a card if a physical change in the inmate's appearance is a matter of their own choice and the change occurs within six months of the initial request for the issuance of a new or replacement card. An inmate will not be charged for replacement of a card because of a physical change in the inmate's appearance over which the inmate has no control."

Furthermore, every ID card is printed with the following warning statement on the back of it: "An identification card must be carried on your person at all times, with the following exception. During working hours, the card must be left with the officer or supervisor in charge of your department. It will be returned to you when you leave your place of employment. Do not under any circumstances leave your place of work assignment without taking this card with you. Loss of this card must be reported to the Captain's office immediately. Non-conforming with the above rules relating to the use of this identification card will result in loss of privileges or other punishment."

As I stated at the beginning of my writing, the prison community is not much different from any other community, in or around the world. If we are forgetful, irresponsible, or don't care about rules and regulations, and we decide to walk around the prison perimeters without our ID cards. We can get pull over by any officer at any given time, an if we don't have our ID card on us upon officer's request, we can be issue a 115 Rules Violation Report (RVR), just in the same manner in which you (the reader of this book) can get a ticket for driving without a license in the free world.

Our ID cards enable us to function appropriately within these walls, just as your driver's licenses allow you to function correctly in the free world. Therefore, be safe and don't forget your ID at home.

Isaac Morquecho

Table of Contents

Photographs

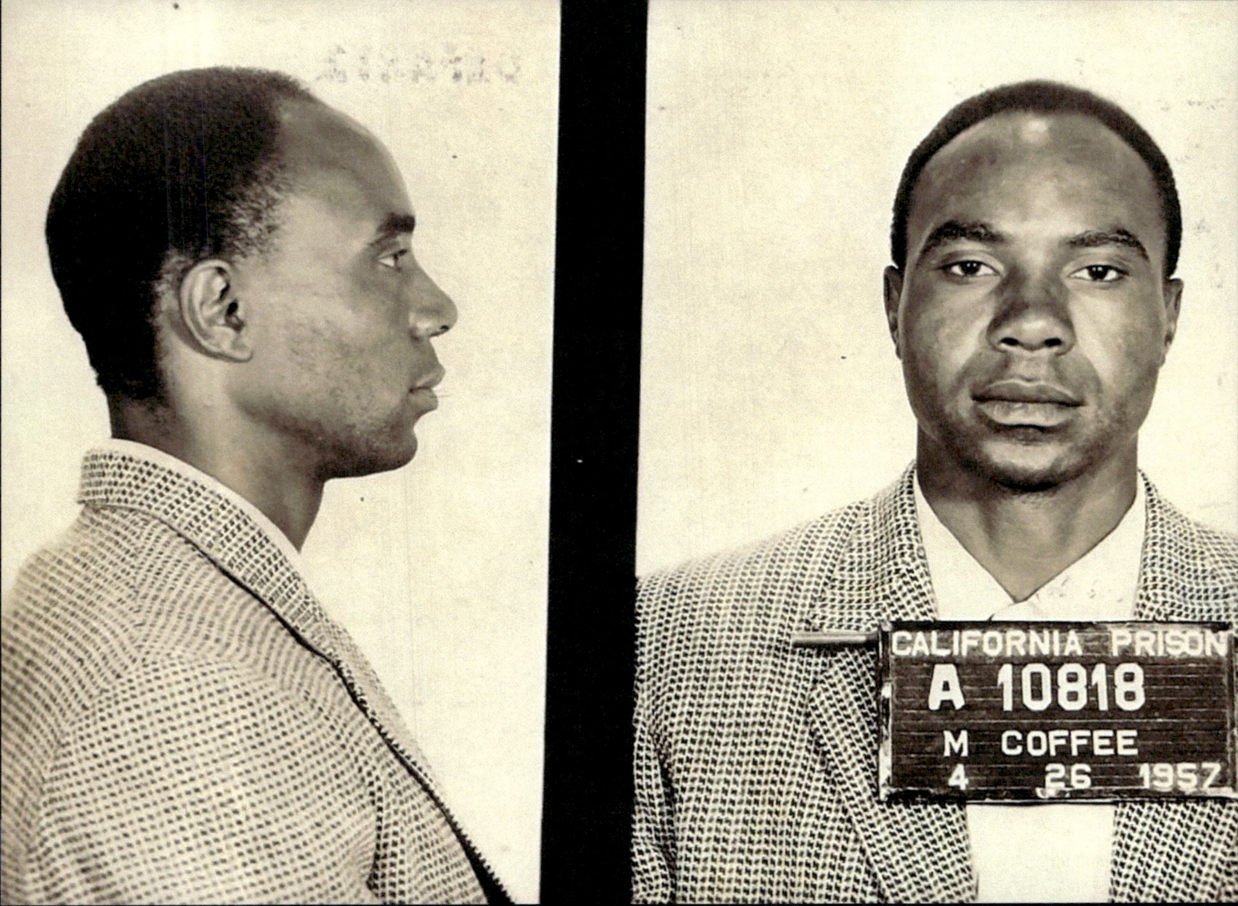

Name: Melvin Leroy Coffee

Height: 70

Weight: 165

Born: 1936

CALIFORNIA PRISON
A 11324
G HAMPTON
4 4 1957

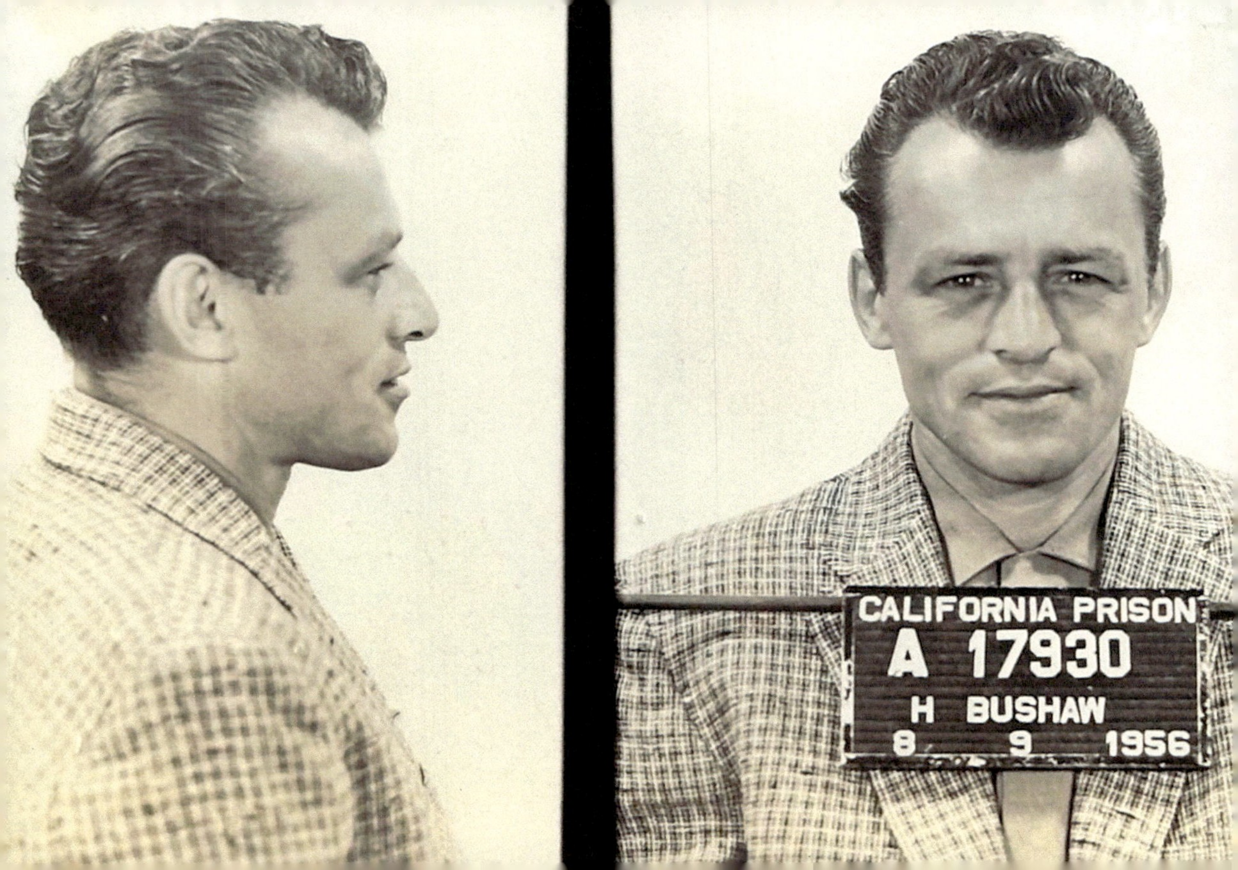
CALIFORNIA PRISON
A 17930
H BUSHAW
8 9 1956

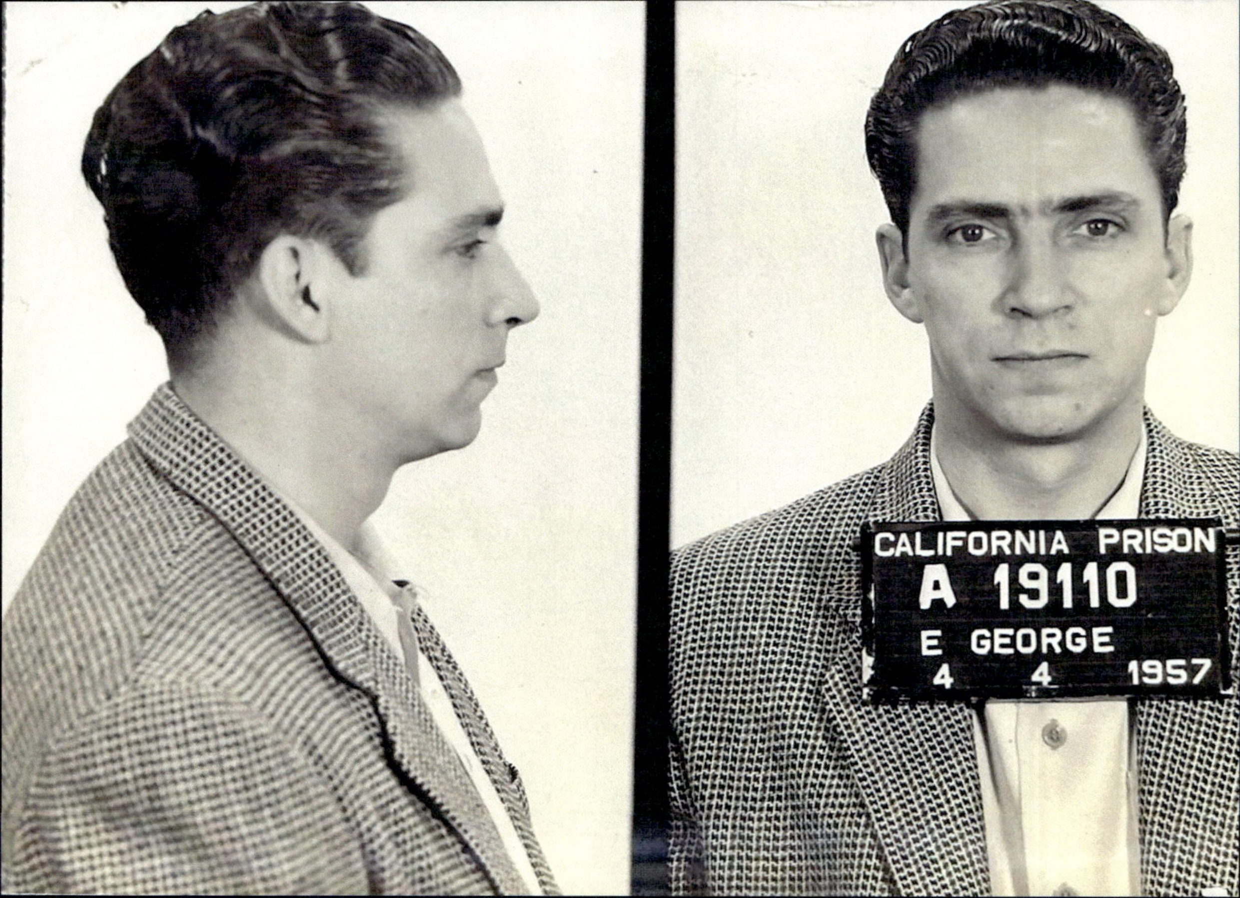

Name: Everette L. George

Height: 69

Weight: 137

Born: 1921

Name: Joseph Sullivan

Height: 66.5

Weight: 142

Born: 1906

Name: Clyde Castle May

Height: 74.5

Weight: 148

Born: 1905

Name: Lester Nunes

Height: 66

Weight: 146

Born: 1903

CALIFORNIA PRISON
A23835
E JENKINS
8 11 1955

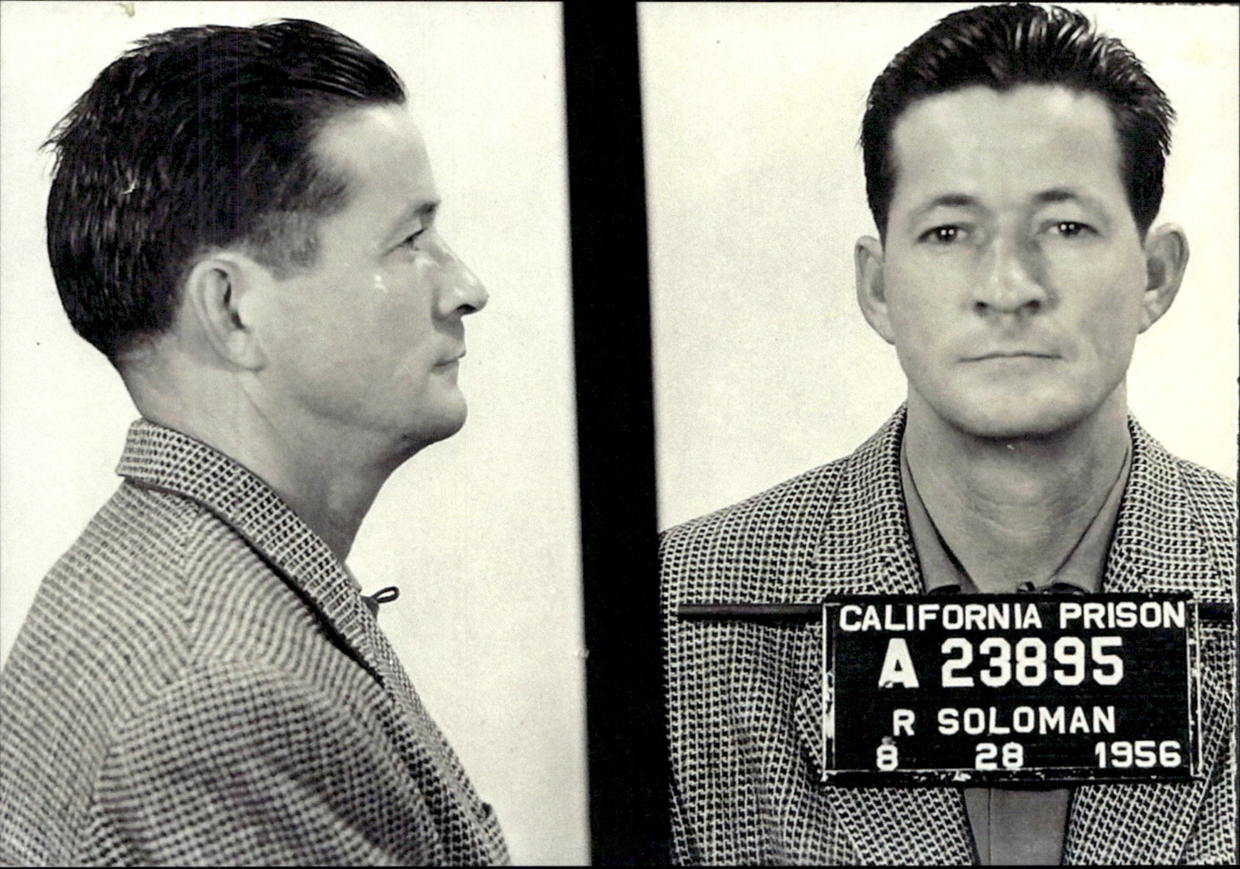

Name: Ralph Waldo Solomon

Height: 71

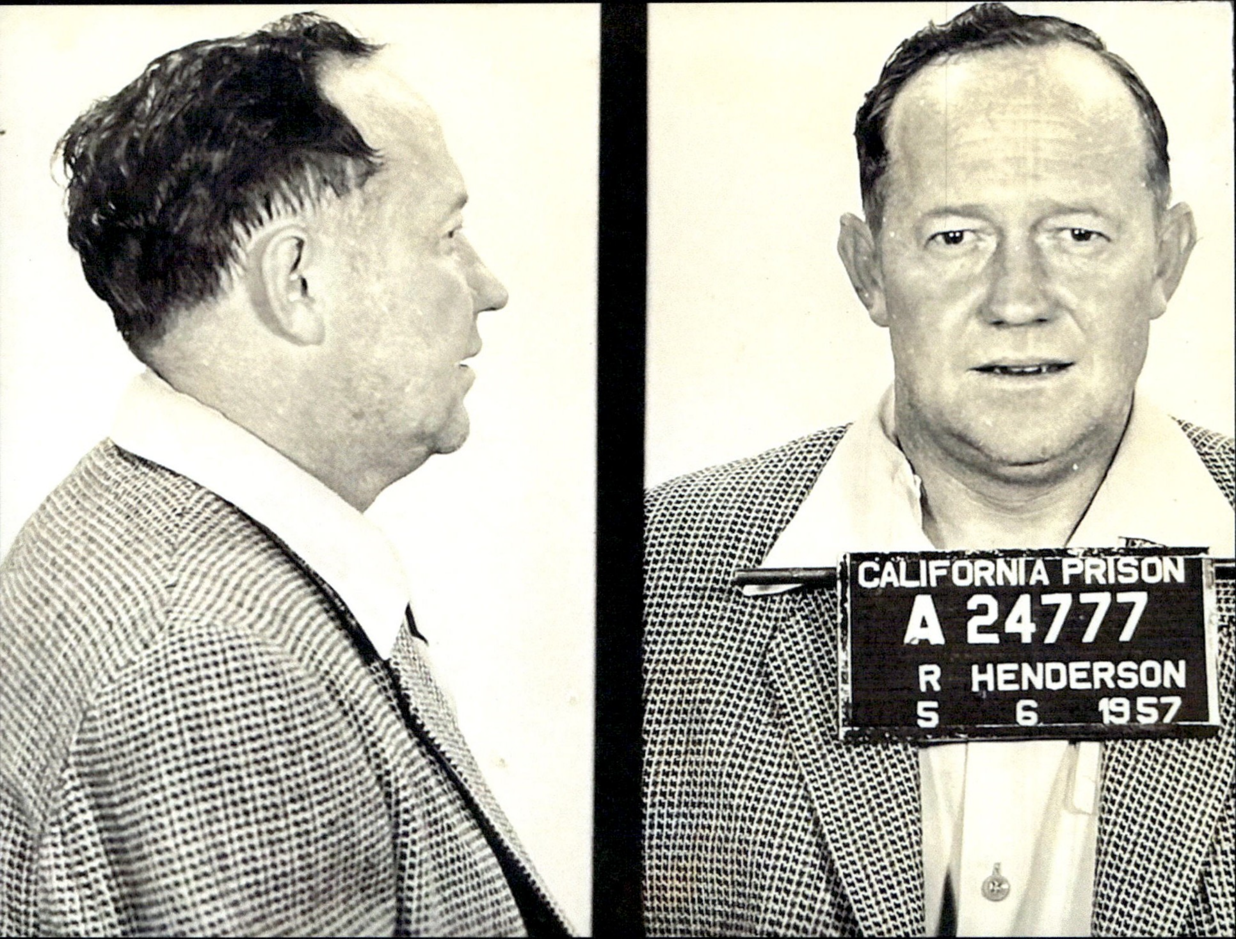

Name: Ralph Emmet Henderson

Height: 68

Weight: 160

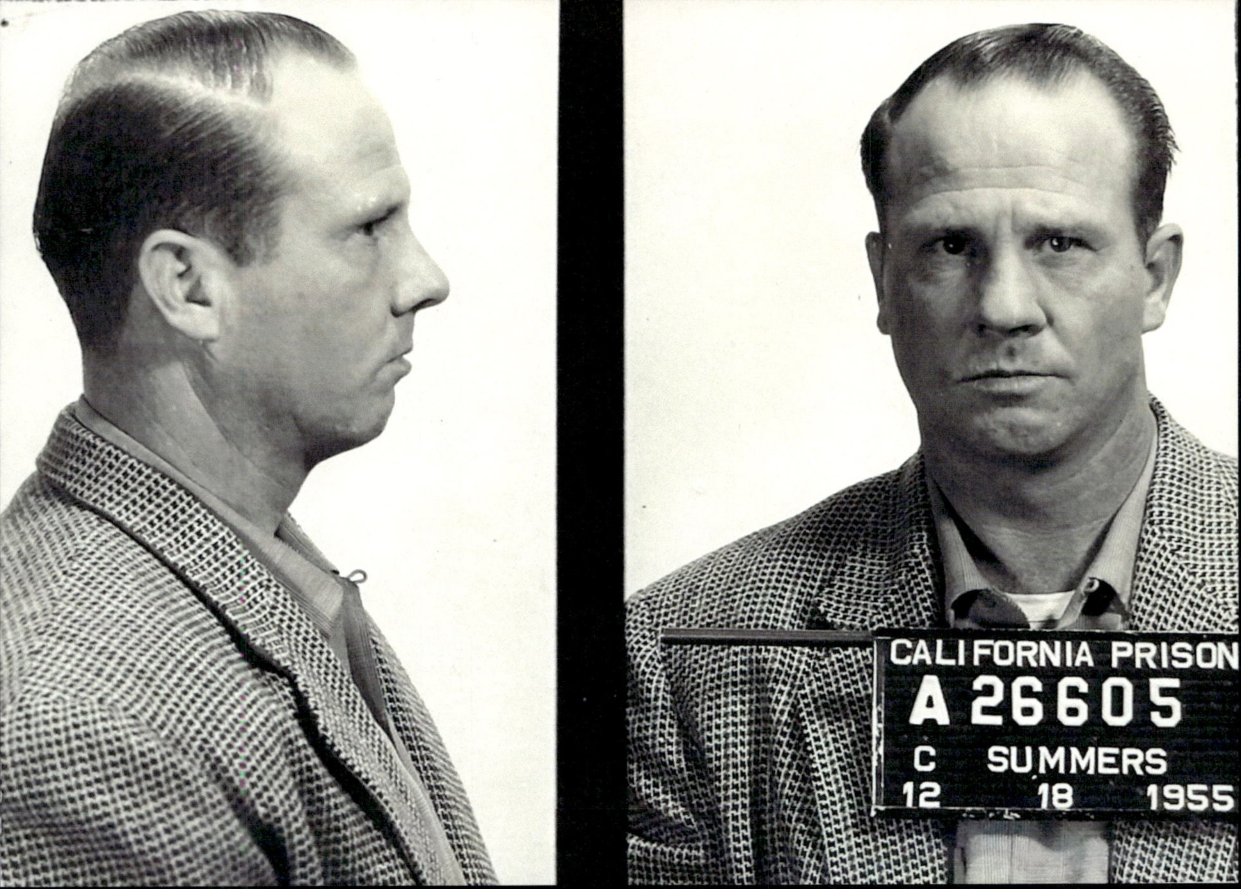

Name: Carl O'Dell Summers

Height: 70

Weight: 185

Born: 1905

Name: John Wesley Smithart

Height: Unknown

Weight: Unknown

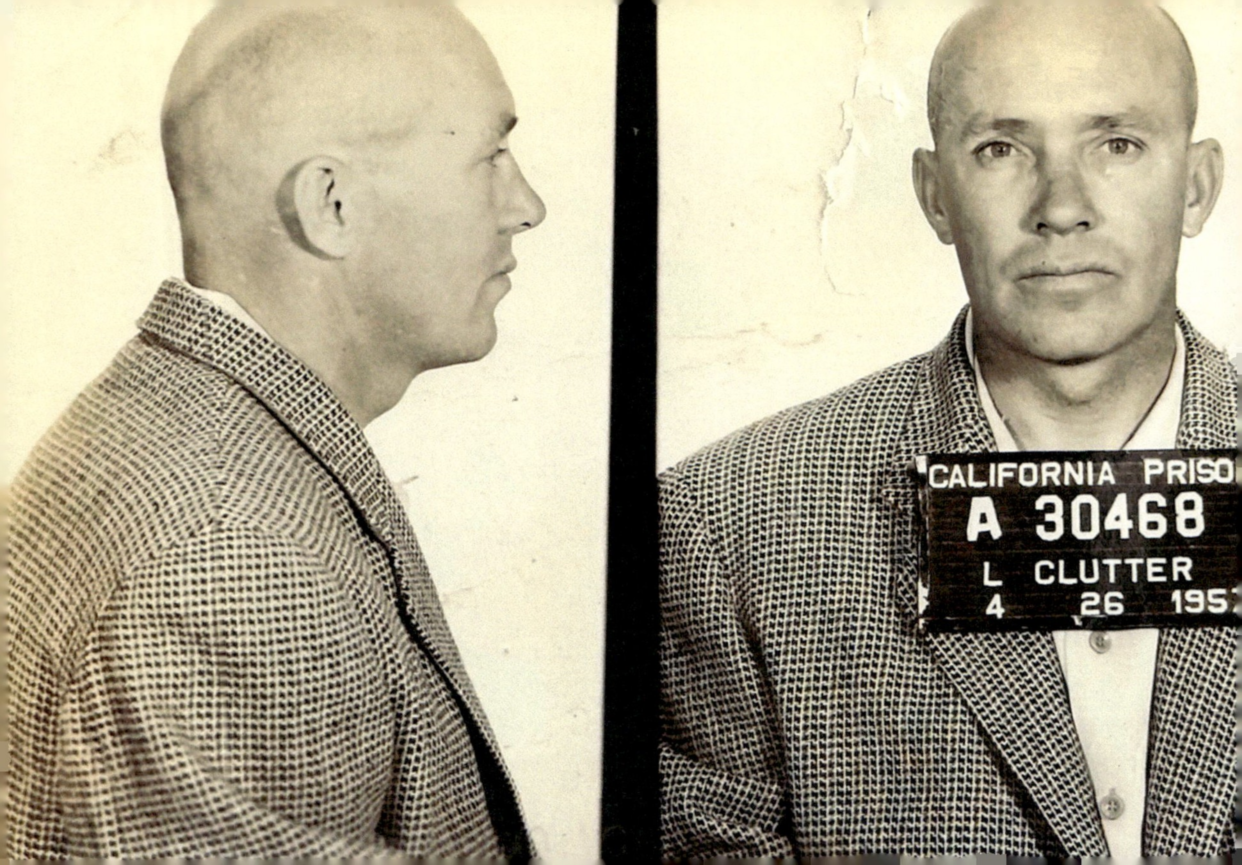
CALIFORNIA PRISO
A 30468
L CLUTTER
4 26 1957

Name: Harold A. Langdon

Height: 69

Weight: 147

Born: 1928

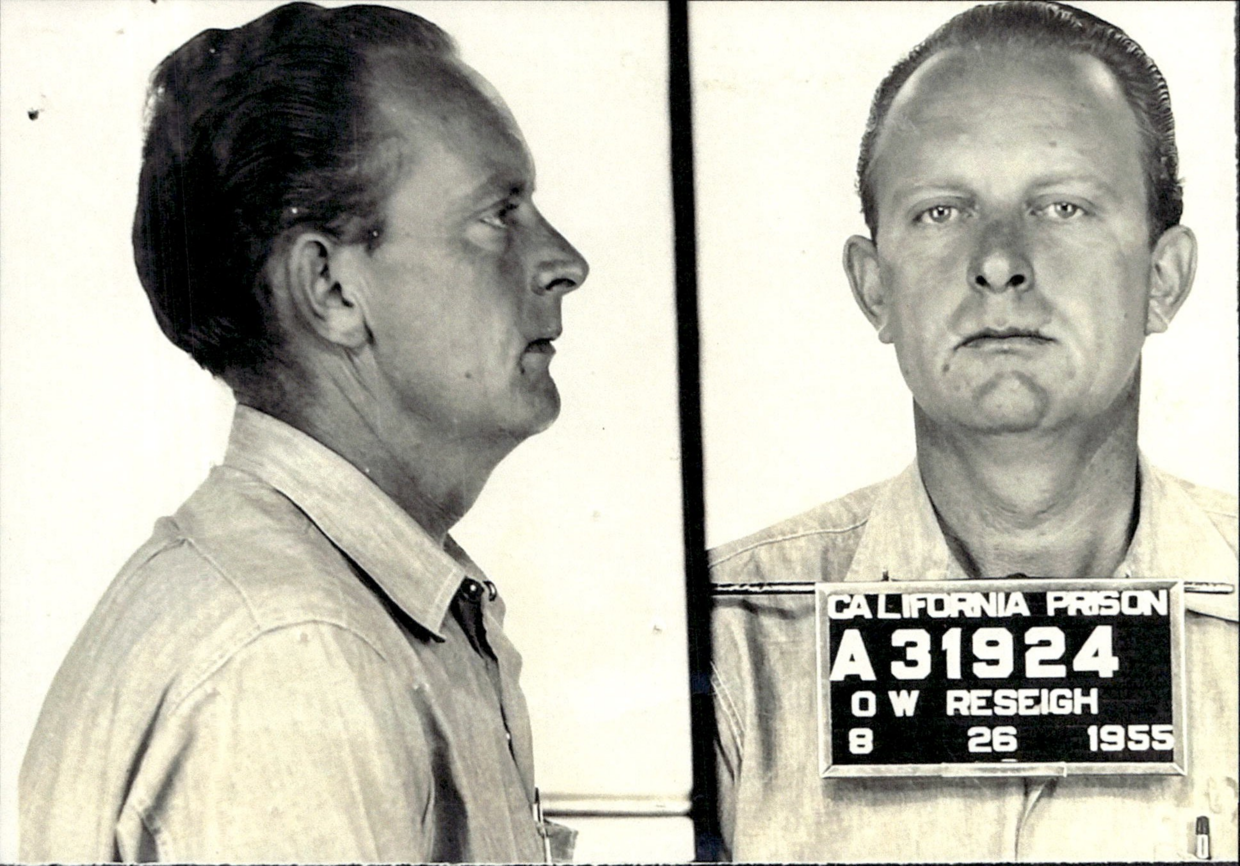

Name: Oscar W. Reseigh Jr.

Height: 70

Weight: 180

Born: 1905

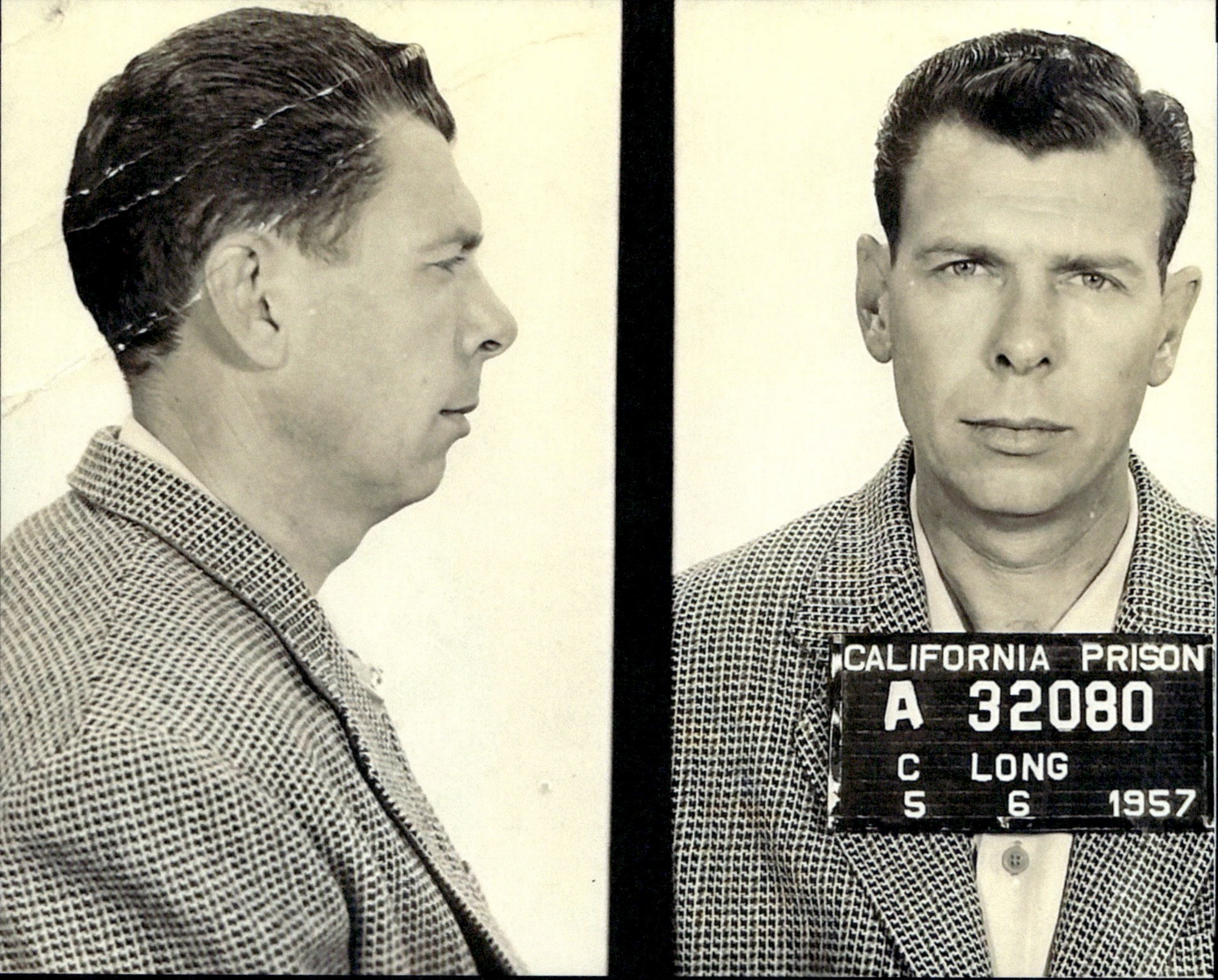

Name: Carl D. Long

Height: 69.5

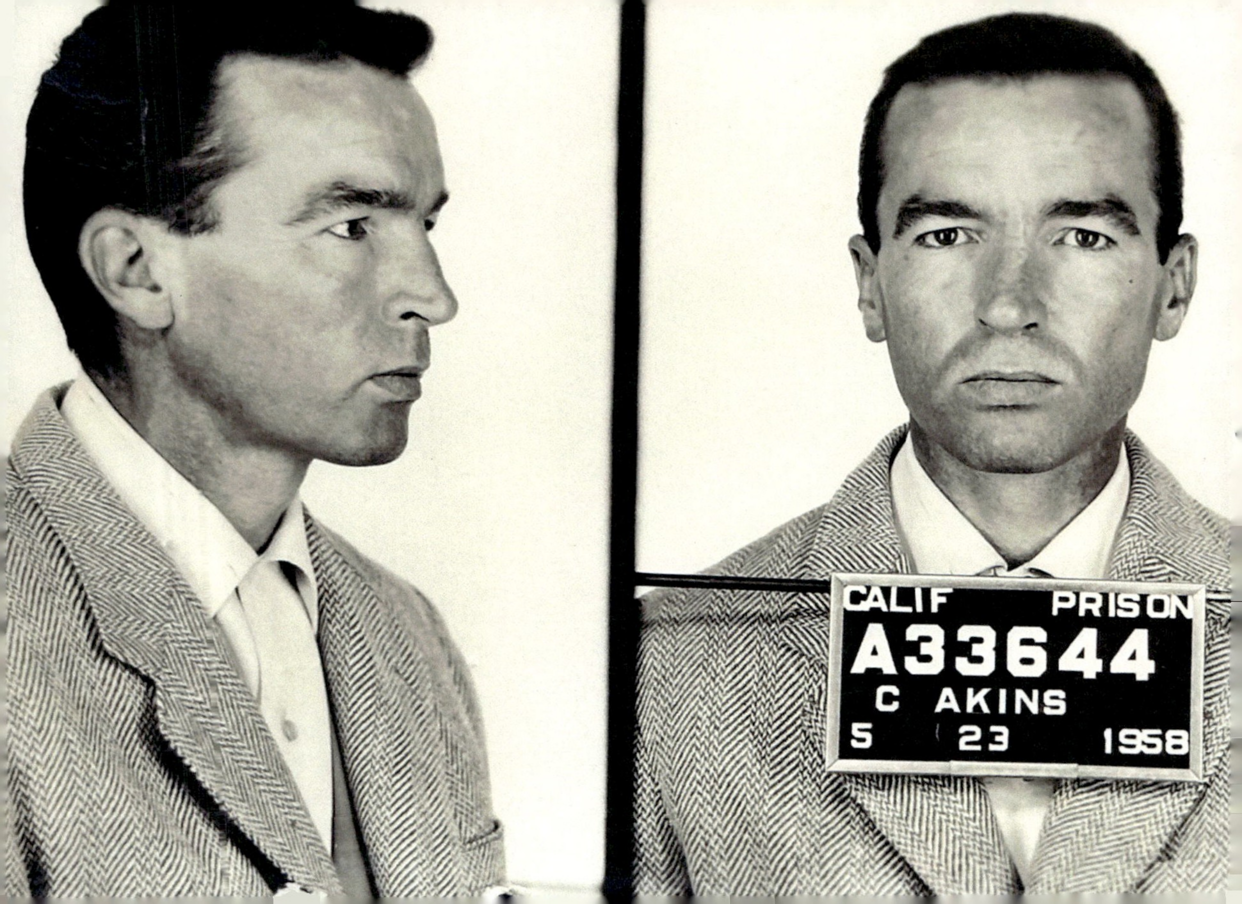
CALIF PRISON
A33644
C AKINS
5 23 1958

Name: Robert Grover Harrison

Height: 71

Weight: 153

Born: 1912

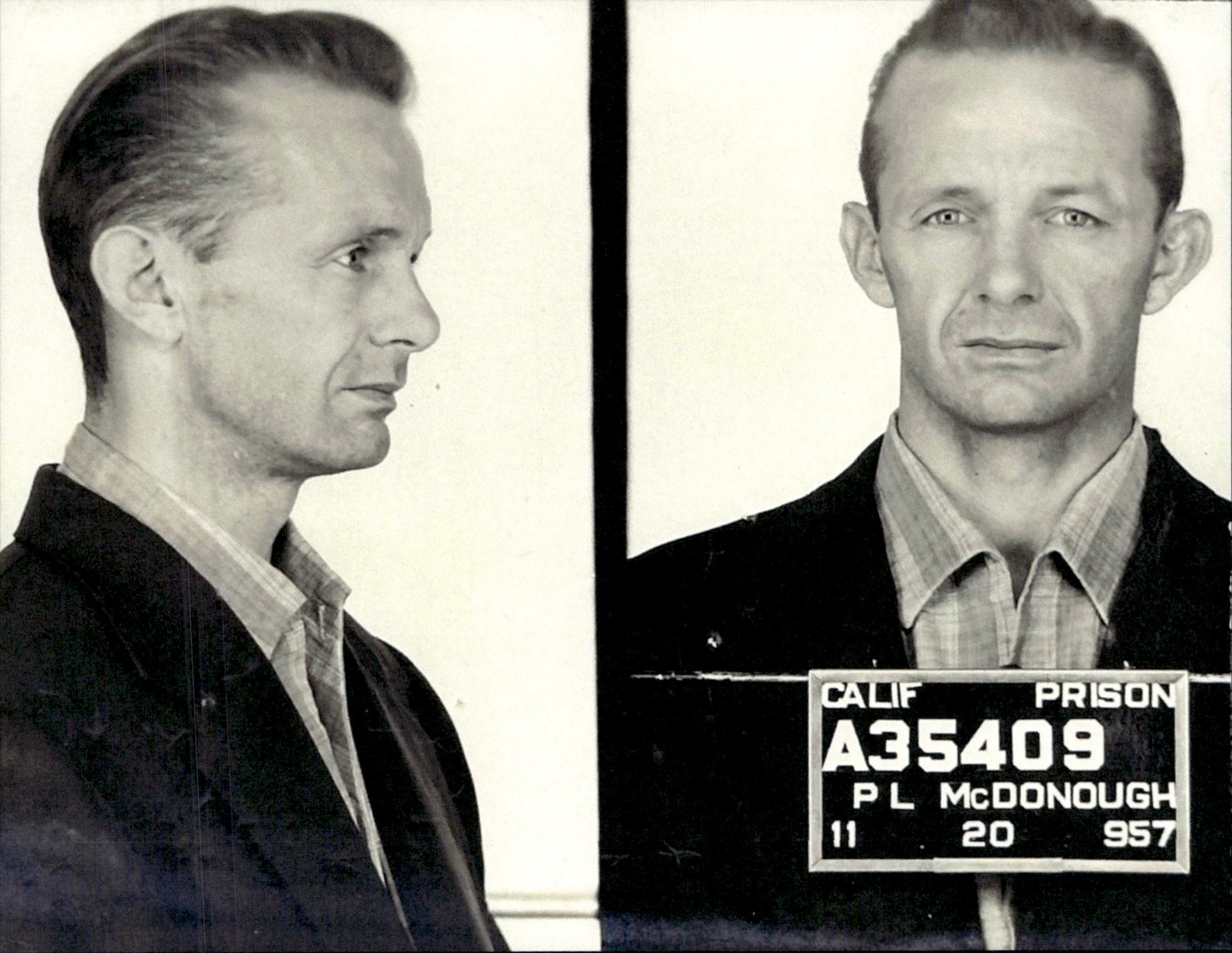

Name: Patrick Leland McDonough

Height: 68

Weight: 142

Born: 1904

Name: Sewell Dewey Noble

Height: 67.5

Weight: 190

Born: 1904

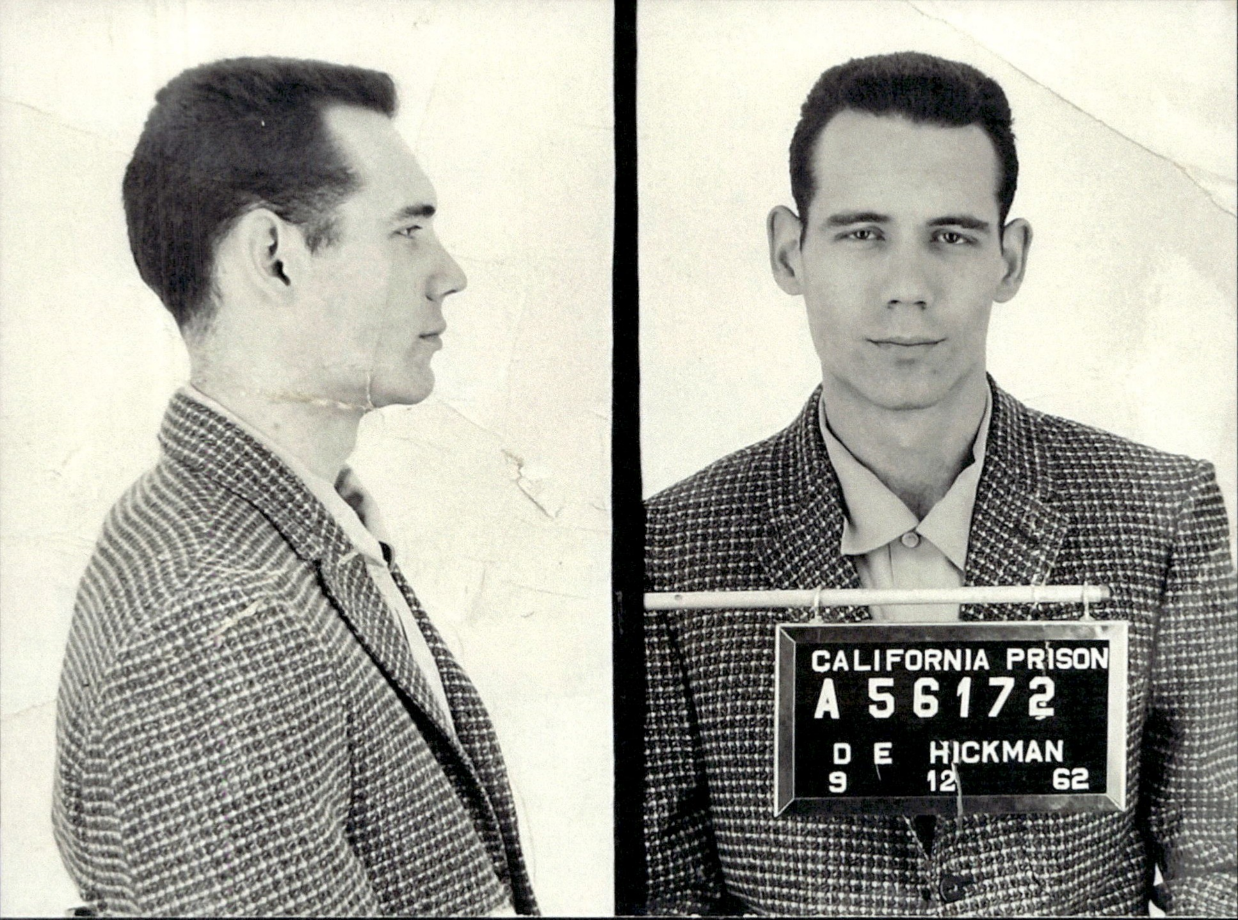

Name: Doug E. Hickman

Height: Unknown

Weight: Unknown

Born: Unknown

Name: Edward Gary Billon

Height: 65.5

Weight: 124

Name: William Arthur De Bowe

Height: 73

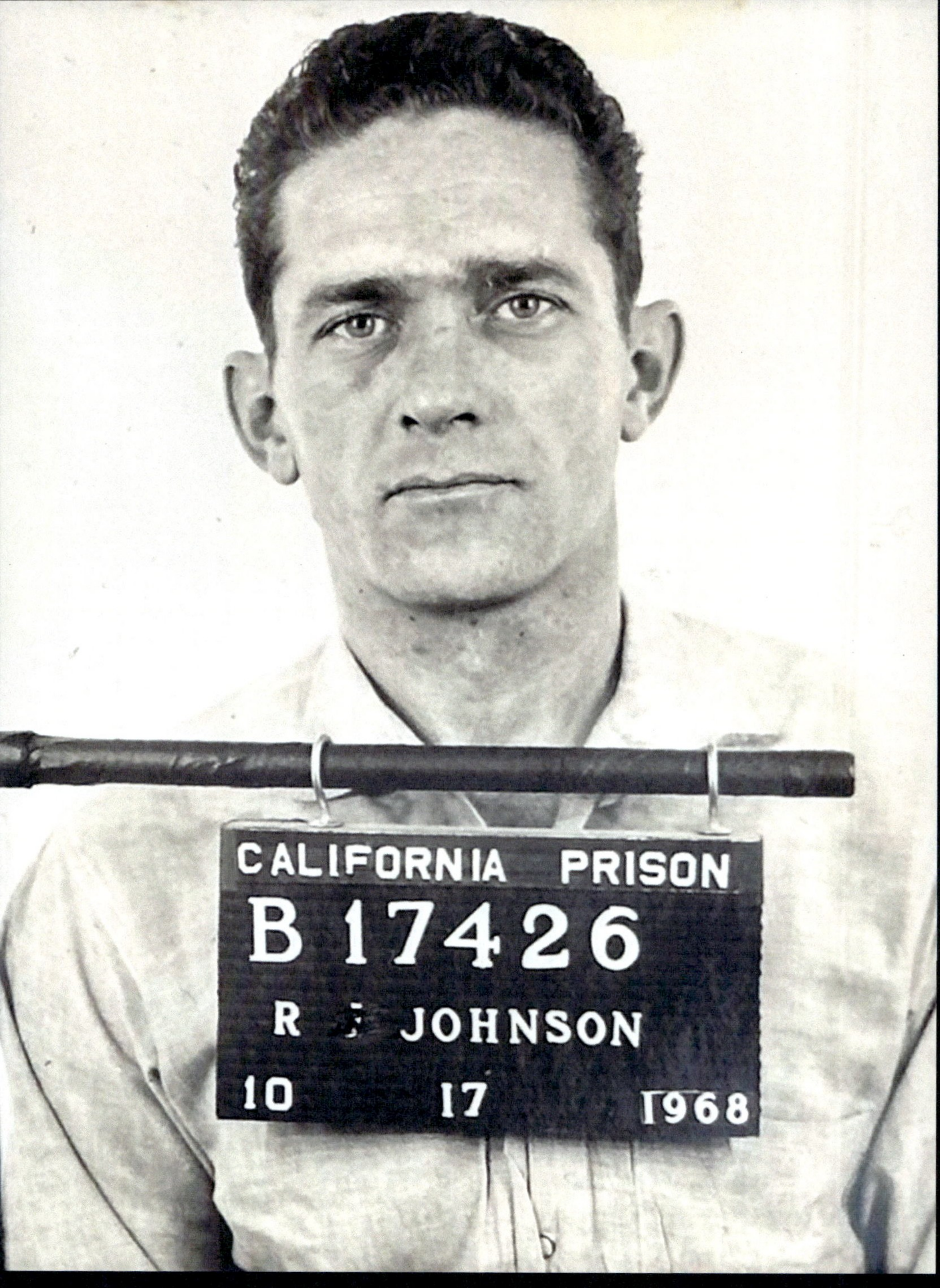

Name: Robert J. Johnson

Height: 69

Weight: 164

Born: 10-27-1935

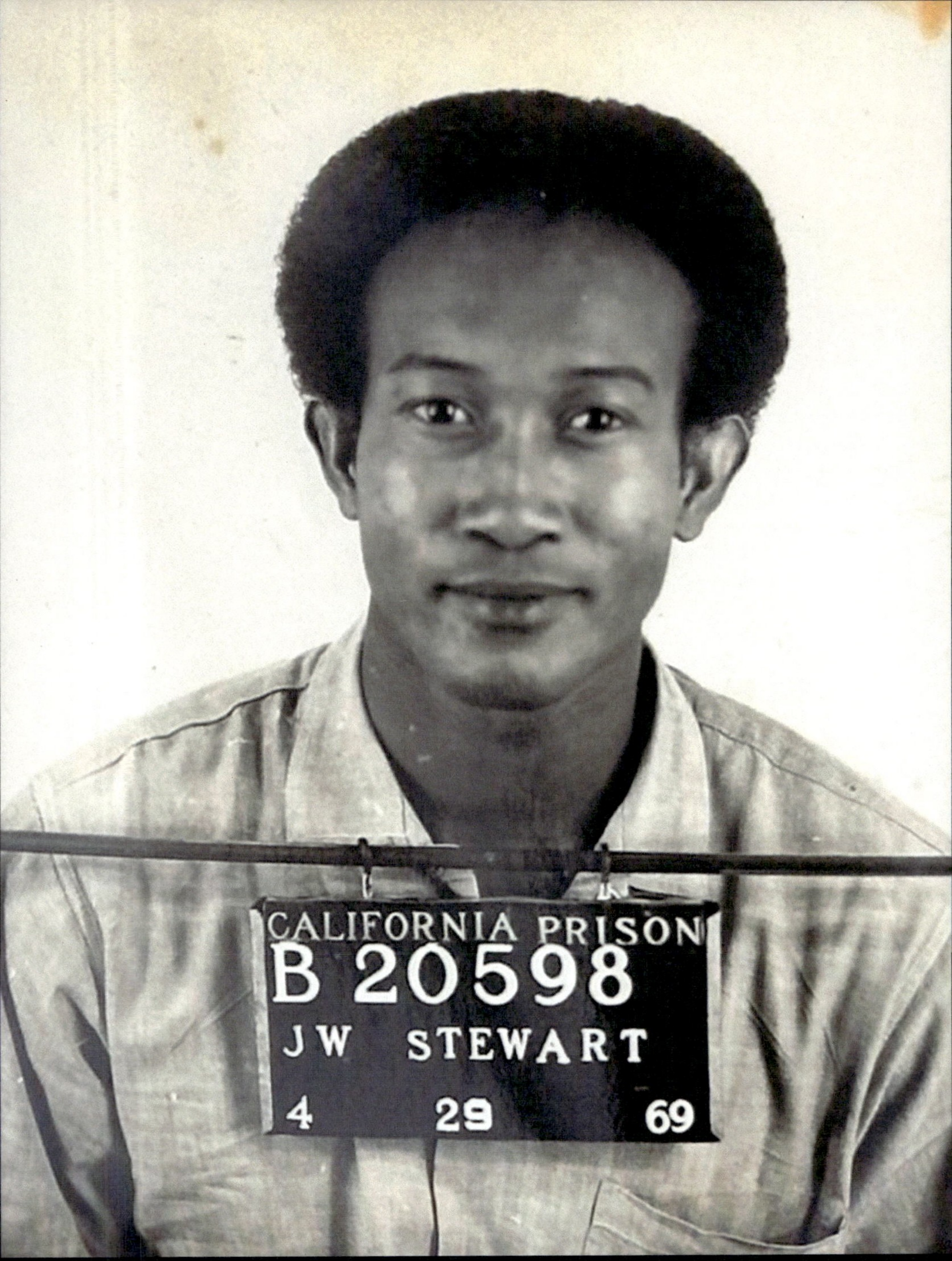

Name: James Weldon Stewart

Height: 69

Weight: 140

About the Author

Eric has emerged as a highly accomplished investor and Day Trader, engaging in trading activities with a substantial value of stocks annually. He enjoys the status of a dedicated husband and father, being blessed with four wonderful daughters who hold a special place in his heart. Eric's existence revolves around upholding the virtues of a devout Christian, a devoted husband, and a caring father guided by the grace of God. His journey has been transformative, considering his challenging upbringing, and he now stands as an illustrious testament to the boundless possibilities achievable through faith in God.

Eric joined a criminal street gang as a teenager, and he was eventually arrested and put in a cage at the Long Beach City Jail. He dropped out of Jordan High School in Long Beach, California, in the 10th grade. Eric eventually got on the right path by the grace of God and obtained his GED the same month that he would have graduated. He joined the United States Coast Guard at 18, and after four years of faithful service, he was honorably discharged.

The following is an excerpt from his autobiography: "California Prison Confessions." "It was a typical beautiful summer night in Long Beach, California, and the three young teens fighting in the musty garage starkly contrasted the night's serenity. A teen called Bones was thrown against a wall, and a muscular teenager nicknamed E Double (me) rushed towards him and violently punched him in his lower back. Another youth named Tim Loc held Bones against the wall during this attack. E Double's knuckles landed with a thick-sounding thud as Bones grimaced and moaned in pain from each successive blow.

There's a look of pain and fear in Bone's eyes as E Double mercilessly lands blow after blow to his kidneys. E Double has spent years hitting the heavy bag in his garage, so his punches are devastating for his age. The beating lasted a minute, and the two teens stopped attacking the unfortunate victim. Amazingly, they all shook hands and embraced each other. We were all friends, and this was our modest gang initiation into our small clique called 'Six Feet Under.'"

Our tiny neighborhood gang in North Long Beach, California, had several members of various races: White, Black, and Hispanic. The definition of a criminal street gang according to the California Penal Code is as follows: "As used in this chapter, 'criminal street gang' means any ongoing organization, association, or group of three or more persons, whether formal or informal, having as one of its primary activities the commission of one or more of the criminal acts…having a common name or common identifying sign or symbol, and whose members individually or collectively engage in or have engaged in a pattern of criminal gang activity," California Penal Code 186.22(f).

Some of our associates committed serious crimes such as burglaries, drug sales, stealing cars, carrying guns, vandalism, and assaulting people. Although we were nothing but young punks, we were a criminal street gang according to the California Penal Code.

The FBI did a study entitled "Street-Gang Mentality: A Mosaic of Remorseless Violence and Relentless Loyalty." I want to quote a relevant part concerning young males who do not have a father or other positive male role models in their lives while growing up: "All gang members lacked male role models in their households, and when they lived with their mothers, they were rarely home because of work schedules. Gang members often lived temporarily with various people. All but one gang member reported that one or more immediate family members had a criminal history or abused drugs. Gangs attracted them because of their loyalty, stability, and sense of group identity."

There is an epidemic in this country of boys masquerading as men who don't take their responsibilities as fathers seriously. Many fathers aren't involved in their children's lives; if they are, they are a horrible example of what a real man should be. One of the main factors in young men ending up in the penal system is the lack of a father or, at the very least, a positive male role model when they were growing up. Absentee fathers are causing society to pay a high price for their selfish and callous actions.

Every day, I strive to be the best dad to the four beautiful daughters God has blessed me with. I live by the motto, "Be the man you needed as a child." I will not allow the actions of physically and emotionally abusive people to define who I am or hinder my advancement in life. You can choose to be bitter or better. I strive for excellence because living well is the best response to abusive people.

Eric Sturgess

God bless you and yours.

Romans 10:9-13

For those seeking to connect with Eric or gather additional insights about his upcoming projects, please visit his official website: EricSturgess.com.

Other Books

Prison Paños: Ink On Cloth

Prison Art Paños

Prison Art Hats

California Prisons: Boxing Program History

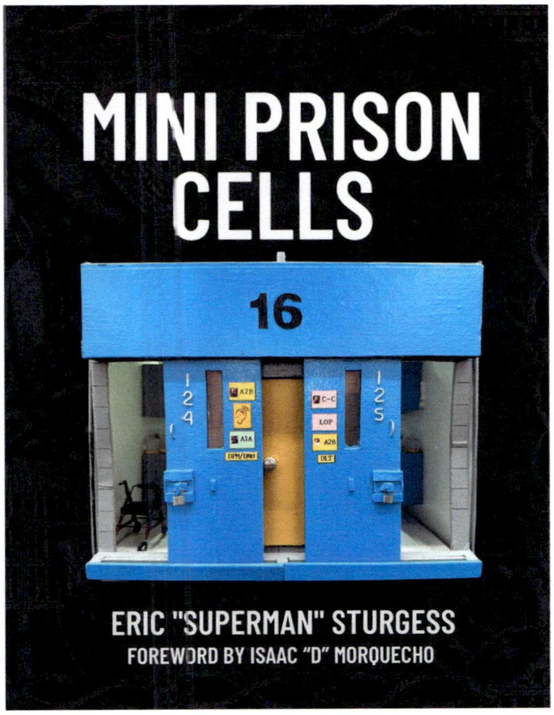

Mini Prison Cells

California Prison Polaroids

Camp Mendenhall: California Juvenile Detention Camp

Imperial Japanese Military Photos 1937

Prison Art Envelopes

Prison Slang Dictionary

U.S. Military Group Photos

Lompoc Federal Prison Inmate Photos 1980

California Prison Photos

Tehachapi Prison Wedding: May 1976

Carlos "Big Fox" Lopez: The Final Sketch

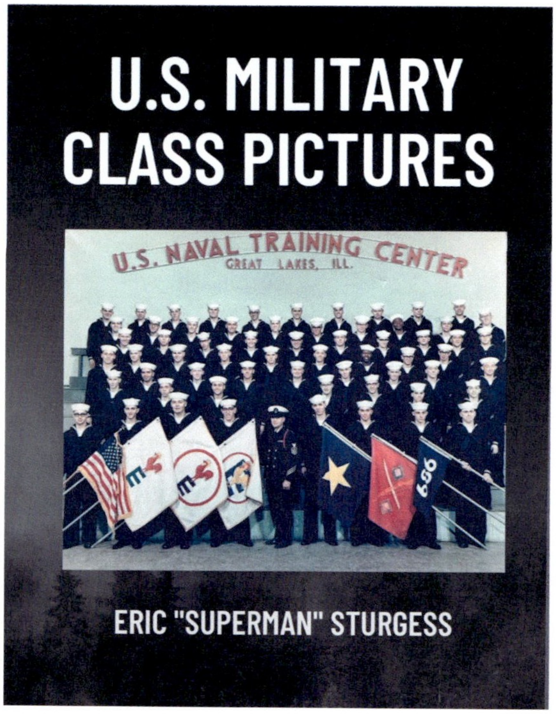

U.S. Military Class Pictures